Water

Fiona Macdonald

FRANKLIN WATTS
A Division of Grolier Publishing
NEW YORK • LONDON • HONG KONG • SYDNEY
DANBURY, CONNECTICUT

Series editor: Helen Lanz
Series designer: John Christopher, WHITE DESIGN
Picture research: Sue Mennell
Illustrators: Peter Bull, Sarah John, and Carolyn Scrace
Consultant: Dot Jackson

First published in 1999 by Franklin Watts

First American edition 2000 by Franklin Watts
A Division of Grolier Publishing
90 Sherman Turnpike
Danbury, CT 06816

Visit Franklin Watts/Children's Press on the Internet at:
http://publishing.grolier.com

A catalog record for this title is available from the Library of Congress

ISBN: 0-531-14543-3 (lib. bdg.)   0-531-15427-0 (pbk.)

Picture credits

Cover: Bruce Coleman Collection/Pacific Stock (main image), Still Pictures/Shehzad Moorani (inset).

Interior Pictures:
Illustrations: Peter Bull: 5, 19, 22-23 (timeline). Sarah John: 6, 7, 8, 9, 10, 13, 17, 20, 21, 22 (top), 23 (top), 24-25, 27. Carolyn Scrace: 14-15.
Photography: AKG 26 'Le Pont d'Argenteuil' Claude Monet, Musée d'Orsay, Paris; Franklin Watts 9 (Ray Moller), 20t (Steve Shott); Robert Harding Picture Library 24; James Davis Travel Photography 12; Rex Features 24; Still Pictures 4-5 (DERA), 11 & 18b (Shehzad Noorani), 19 (Mark Edwards); Thames Water Picture Library/IDS 16, 17; WaterAid 18t (Caroline Penn).

WaterAid is the UK's specialist development charity working with people in developing countries to improve their quality of life through lasting improvement to water, sanitation, and hygiene using skills and practical technologies.

Contents

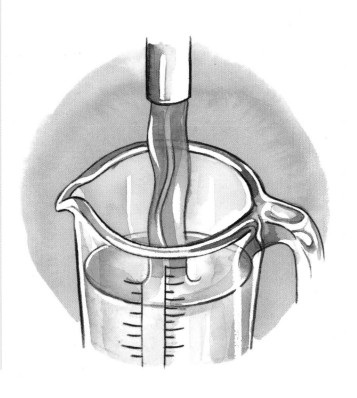

The World of Water

Our world is surrounded by water. Seas, rivers, and lakes cover nearly three-quarters of the earth's surface. Water is frozen in snowfields at the top of high mountains and in huge sheets of ice at the Arctic and Antarctic — the areas around the North and South Poles.

Water All Around

There is water in the air all around us, as well.

We can see it as rain, clouds, and mist.

Scientists call this water all around us the hydrosphere.

Without water, there could be no life on the earth.

Water covers 70 percent of the earth's surface — that is about 145,011,200 square miles (375,550,000 square kilometers). That's a lot of water!

The Water Cycle

All the world's water — the water in rivers and lakes, ponds and puddles, oceans and seas, ice sheets, and clouds — is connected. And it keeps moving all the time. This moving water is called the water cycle.

1. As the sun warms the water on the surface of the sea, rivers, and lakes, it evaporates (turns into water vapor) and rises into the air.

2. The water vapor rises higher, cools, and condenses (turns into a liquid). This liquid forms water droplets. These droplets collect in clouds.

3. As more droplets form, the water falls back down to the earth again as rain.

4. Water runs from the surface of the earth into rivers, which flow back out to sea.

Did you know...

Rain is formed when water droplets in the air cool and condense to create clouds. The droplets join together into larger drops. When the drops get too big and heavy, they fall to the ground as rain, hail, or snow.

An average raindrop measures about 3/4 in (2 mm) across. A water droplet is 100 times smaller.

The Qualities of Water

Water is a clear, colorless liquid. It has no taste or smell. It is formed when two invisible gases, oxygen and hydrogen, join together.

Water Tricks

Water seems to have magical qualities. It can change shape, and it can seem to make things disappear. Try these water tricks for yourself.

YOU CAN TRY THIS!

Changing Shape Part One

1 *Partly fill a plastic bottle with tap water.*

2 *Mark the water level on the side of the bottle with a felt tip pen. Do not put the bottle's lid on.*

3 *Stand the bottle in the freezer (make sure the bottle is upright). Leave it to freeze.*

4 *After 3–4 hours, go back and look at the bottle. What do you see? What has happened to the water?*

Look at the water level.

? **What do you notice about the water when it freezes?**

The water turns from a liquid into a solid (ice). As it does this, it expands (gets bigger) and so takes up more room. This means that the solid water (ice) reaches a higher level in the bottle than the liquid water.

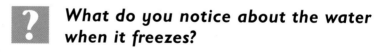

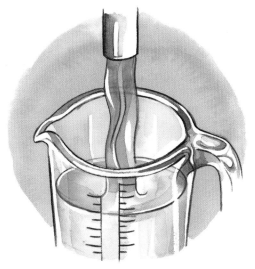

Changing Shape Part Two

1 *Measure 2 cups (500 ml) of water in a measuring cup.*

2 *Pour the water into a saucepan. Ask an adult to boil the water for five minutes.*

ASK AN ADULT

3 *Look carefully at what is happening while the water boils.*

4 *After five minutes, let the water cool. Pour the cooled water back into the measuring cup to measure it again.*

? **Where do you think the water has gone?**

The water has evaporated and risen into the air as steam.

◀ *A small amount of water changes into a large amount of steam.*

Solid, Liquid, Gas

As the temperature changes, water alters its shape and appearance. Water can change into a liquid, a solid, or a gas.

At room temperature, water is a liquid.

When water is cooled to 32°F (0°C), it freezes and becomes ice. Ice is a solid.

When water is heated to 212°F (100°C), it forms clouds of tiny water droplets called water vapor, or steam. Water vapor is a gas.

Water is one of only a few substances that can be found in its three states (solid, liquid, and gas) at temperatures that occur daily.

Water Words

Many different words are used to describe water. Some water words are listed below. See if you can find them in this book, and discover what they mean.

vapor
droplet
evaporate
hydrosphere
dissolve
condensation
steam
ice
water cycle
liquid

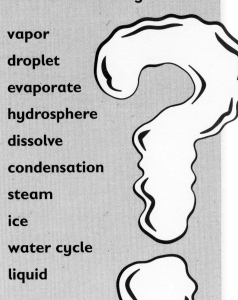

A Disappearing Act

Salt and sugar are both solid substances. They feel rough and gritty.

1 *Put half a teaspoon of salt into a glass of warm water. Stir it well.*

2 *Now put half a teaspoon of sugar into another glass of warm water. Stir it well.*

3 *Look at both glasses. Can you see the salt and sugar?*

4 *Dip a clean finger and thumb in each glass — can you feel the salt and the sugar? They seem to have disappeared.*

5 *Dip your finger into one glass again. Lick your fingertip. Try the liquid in the other glass, too!* **Do not drink the water — just taste it on your fingertips!**

? **What do you find?**

The salt and the sugar cannot be seen, but they are still there. You can taste them in the water.

Dissolving

Salt and sugar are made up of tiny pieces of solids. When they are mixed with water, the tiny pieces get separated from one another and spread through the water. This makes them lose their shape and solid form. We say they have dissolved.

Try This! Now you see it …

Many solids dissolve in water, but not all. See which of the following dissolve in water.

Cocoa powder, instant coffee, baking soda, sugar cubes, sugar crystals, sand.

You will find that some dissolve completely, some dissolve partially, and some do not dissolve at all. Keep a record of what you find.

Water and Us

Water for Life

All living things need water.

Without water, there would be no people, animals, or plants.

We can survive for weeks without food. But without water we would die after only three or four days.

To stay healthy, adults need to drink about ½ gallon (2 liters) of water a day.

Over two-thirds of our bodies are water.

There is water in our tears, sweat, saliva, and blood. It is in our urine, too.

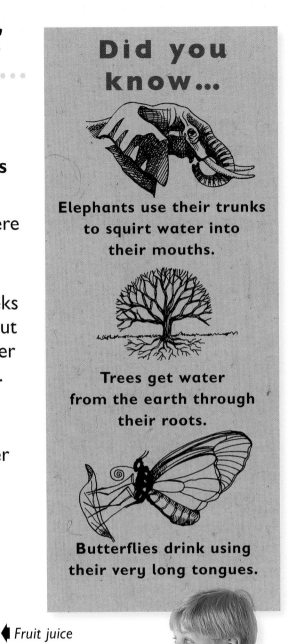

Did you know...

Elephants use their trunks to squirt water into their mouths.

Trees get water from the earth through their roots.

Butterflies drink using their very long tongues.

◀ Pure water is very good for you!

◀ Fruit juice contains water and concentrated fruit juice.

▶ Soft drinks contain water, sugar, gas, and flavorings.

Try This! Water Dragons

Have you heard stories about dragons that breathe out fire? Our bodies do something just as amazing. We breathe out water vapor! Usually we cannot see the water we breathe out. It is invisible.

Follow these instructions to see the water vapor for yourself.

1 Find a mirror.

2 Put it in the refrigerator for an hour to chill it.

3 Take the mirror out and hold it near your mouth. Breathe on it hard.

4 What happens? The mirror mists over.

When the warm water vapor in our breath hits the cold mirror, it forms tiny droplets. This is called condensation. We can see it.

You could write a story or paint a picture about the adventures of a dragon who breathed out water, not fire. If you find it hard to start, you could complete this limerick:

"There once was a dragon called James
Who breathed out water, not flames ..."

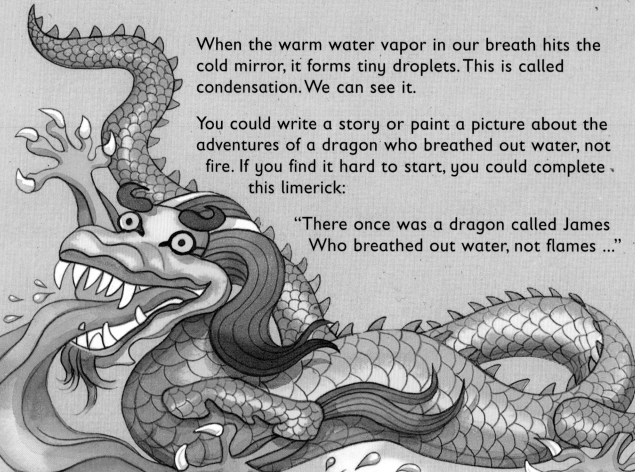

Floods and Droughts

When too much rain falls, it causes floods. There are two different kinds of floods: flash floods and broadscale floods. Both kinds of floods cause serious damage to buildings and crops on farmland. People are often drowned.

Floods

Flash floods are caused by sudden, severe storms. Too much rain falls too quickly for rivers and drains to carry it away.

This woman is trying to save some of her possessions after this broadscale flood in Bangladesh.

Rivers rise over their banks and flood streets and houses with water. As water gushes over the land, it can cause dangerous mudslides. People, animals, and buildings can be swept away.

Broadscale floods are caused by days of heavy rainfall over a wide area. Slowly, rivers and drains fill up, and water covers the land as far as the eye can see.

Floods make clean water dirty and dangerous to drink. After a flood, people can catch diseases from dirty drinking water. Severe floods destroy food crops growing in fields. Sometimes, people starve.

Droughts

When less rain falls than usual over a certain time period, there is a shortage of water. This is called a drought.

The ground becomes dry and cracked. Plants shrivel and die. People and animals have nothing to drink. Sometimes they die, too.

No one knows for sure why droughts occur. They may be caused by natural changes in ocean currents, which affect the weather.

Another cause might be air pollution, such as smoke from factories or exhaust fumes from cars. Some scientists believe such pollution leads to changes in the world's weather patterns.

➥ *In a drought, plants die and their roots shrivel. Soil becomes loose and blows away in dust storms. The earth beneath becomes dry and cracked.*

Did you know...

Some floods are very useful. For thousands of years, people living in Egypt relied on regular floods from the Nile River to bring life-giving water to their fields.

In the Sahel region of Africa (the area to the south of the Sahara Desert), there has been a drought for the past 30 years.

NOAH AND THE FLOOD

Ancient legends from the Middle East, written down in the Bible, tell the story of Noah and his ark:

God warned Noah that there would soon be a terrible flood. He told him to build an ark — a big boat — to shelter in. When God gave the word, Noah told his family to go into the ark. He rounded up pairs of all the different animals he could find, and loaded them aboard, two by two.

Then the rain fell. It rained without stopping for 40 days and 40 nights. When it stopped raining, all the houses and fields were covered with water. The flood was so deep, it even covered the trees. When Noah looked out from the ark, all he could see was water. The whole world had been drowned.

Noah was in despair. What could he do? Then he had a bright idea. He would send a look-out. He released one of the ravens to fly over the floodwaters. If it did not come back, Noah would know that it had found a tree to roost in.

When the raven returned, Noah's heart sank. The bird had not found anywhere to perch. This meant the floodwaters were not falling. Had God let him down? Would he and his ark-load of people and animals die in the flood, after all?

Later, Noah plucked up his courage and decided to try again. This time, he sent a dove to explore. Imagine his joy when she returned carrying an olive branch in her beak. She had found it sticking up out above the floodwater. Olive trees never grow very tall, so Noah realized that the water must at last be draining away.

One sunny morning, Noah felt the bottom of the ark scraping against something solid. A few days later, he could see dry land! The ark had come to rest at the top of a high mountain, and the floodwaters had all gone away. He was saved!

Today, people still point out a high mountain, called Mount Ararat, in Turkey, as the place where Noah's ark ran aground after the flood.

Water Creatures

Creatures that live in water include some of the oldest living species on the earth. They first appeared over 500 million years ago. Some water creatures live in salty water, like seas and oceans; others live in fresh water, like rivers and ponds.

Some of the best-known water creatures are not fish at all. Whales, dolphins, and porpoises are mammals, like dogs, cats — and ourselves!

Number Work

Using the information on these pages, try to work out the following math puzzles.

✪ How far apart do the highest and lowest sea creatures live?

✪ The blenny is the slowest fish. It travels at $1/2$ mph (0.8 kph). How much faster does a swordfish travel?

✪ A pygmy goby weighs only $5/100$ ounces (1.5 grams). How many would you get if you asked for $3^{1}/_{2}$ ounces (100 grams) of them?

✪ How much does a blue whale weigh per foot (meter)?

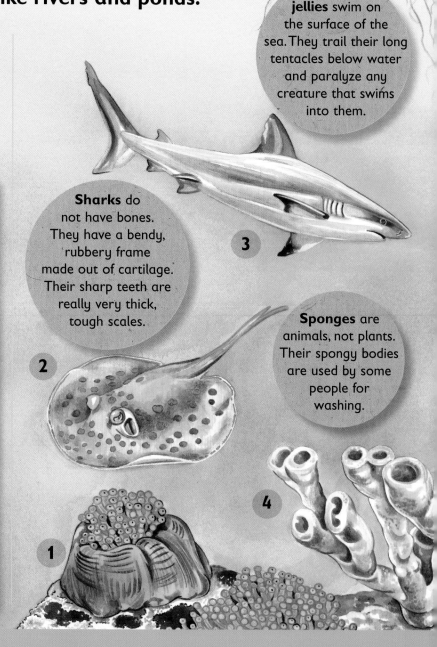

Sea jellies swim on the surface of the sea. They trail their long tentacles below water and paralyze any creature that swims into them.

Sharks do not have bones. They have a bendy, rubbery frame made out of cartilage. Their sharp teeth are really very thick, tough scales.

Sponges are animals, not plants. Their spongy bodies are used by some people for washing.

1. Sea anemone   3. Shark   5. Sea jellies

2. Ray   4. Sponge

14

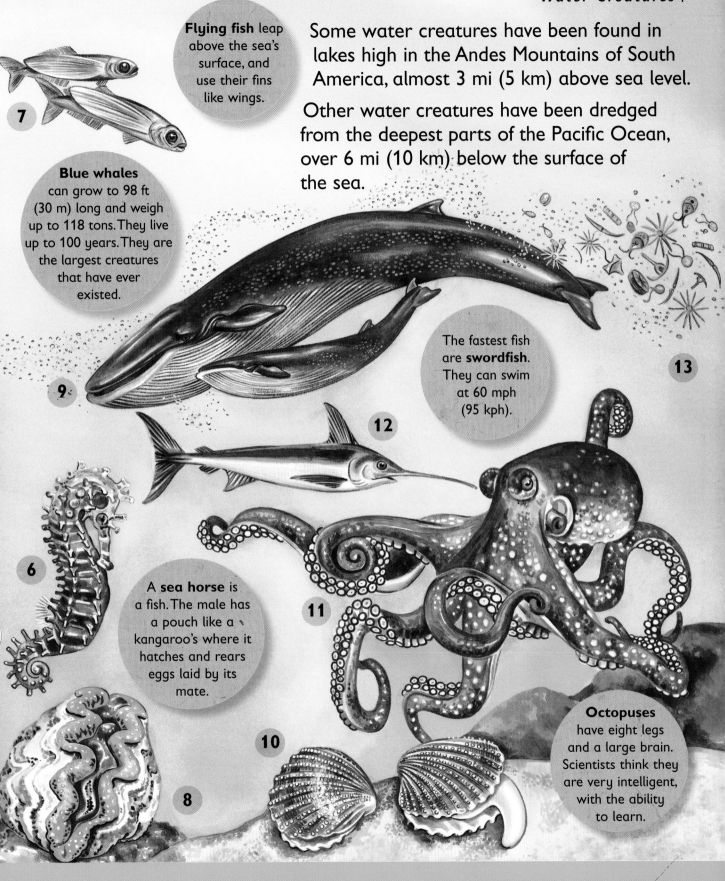

Flying fish leap above the sea's surface, and use their fins like wings.

7

Some water creatures have been found in lakes high in the Andes Mountains of South America, almost 3 mi (5 km) above sea level.

Other water creatures have been dredged from the deepest parts of the Pacific Ocean, over 6 mi (10 km) below the surface of the sea.

Blue whales can grow to 98 ft (30 m) long and weigh up to 118 tons. They live up to 100 years. They are the largest creatures that have ever existed.

9

The fastest fish are **swordfish**. They can swim at 60 mph (95 kph).

13

12

6

A **sea horse** is a fish. The male has a pouch like a kangaroo's where it hatches and rears eggs laid by its mate.

11

10

8

Octopuses have eight legs and a large brain. Scientists think they are very intelligent, with the ability to learn.

6. Sea horse   8. Clam   10. Cockle   12. Swordfish   13. Plankton

7. Flying fish   9. Blue whale   11. Octopus

15

Clean Water, Dirty Water

For many people, getting clean water is easy. They simply turn on a tap and water runs out, at any time of the day or night. They are very lucky — they live in countries that have safe, modern water supplies.

Drinking Water

It takes a lot of work to provide clean water that is safe to drink.

Rain is collected in reservoirs, or taken from rivers and lakes. It is pumped to a water-treatment plant. Used water from homes and industry is also returned there. At the plant, all the water passes through many different stages.

▲ There are two kinds of filter beds at a water-treatment plant. The rectangular beds clean water from reservoirs, rivers, and lakes. The round beds clean water recycled from houses.

◀ Water is filtered through gravel to clean it.

The water is filtered many times to remove poisonous chemicals and tiny bits of plants, dirt and grit. Bright ultraviolet light is also shined into the water to kill germs.

Safe levels of disinfectants, such as chlorine, are sometimes added to the water. These kill any germs that might get into the water as it is piped underground to and from homes.

The water is tested before it leaves the treatment plant, to make sure it is pure and clean.

▲ *Water is tested throughout the cleaning process.*

After it has been cleaned, the water is pumped along large pipes called water mains. These are hidden deep under city streets and under fields in the countryside.

Smaller pipes carry the water from the main pipes to homes.

Try This! Save Water

Pure, clean water is precious. We should not waste it. Here is how we can all help save water.

Be sure to turn taps off carefully so they do not drip.

When you brush your teeth, turn the tap off: don't let the water run.

Take a shower! Showering uses less water than it takes to fill a bath.

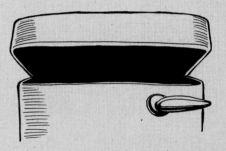

Ask an adult to put a brick in your toilet tank. This reduces the amount of water used every time the toilet is flushed.

Use cool, leftover dishwashing water for watering the garden. Collect rain for watering gardens in a water barrel.

Ask if water-saving programs on washing machines can be used.

◀ *This pipe carries water from the water main to the house.*

Keeping It Clean

Some people do not live close to clean, safe water supplies. There are no pipes bringing water to their houses. They have to walk long distances each day to fetch water from a well. They may have to get their water from rivers and streams that are polluted.

Today, people in many developing countries work hard to provide clean water for everyone. They build wells and water pumps in villages, and find ways of keeping water supplies free from pollution.

◀ In Africa, women spend hours every day carrying heavy jugs of water from the nearest river back to their homes.

◀ Charities such as WaterAid share information with villagers about how to keep clean and dirty water supplies separate.

Waterpower

For thousands of years, people have used the energy of running water to make machines work.

Water is a good source of power. Using waterpower does not cause pollution. Because water can be used over and over again, it is called a renewable source of energy. Today, engineers are trying to invent new ways of using waterpower.

▶ *This waterwheel on a farm in Brazil is being used to power a generator to make electricity. This is called hydroelectricity.*

Examples of Waterpower

In 1881, British engineers designed the world's first hydroelectric power plant. Hydroelectric power stations use water to turn turbines to make electricity.

In 1966, French engineers built the first power station to make electricity from the movement of tides in the sea.

In 1712, British inventors built the first steam engine. Water was heated to make steam (*see p.7*). The pressure of the steam was used to make the engine move.

About 2,000 years ago, Greek builders made waterwheels. The force of the running water in rivers was used to turn the waterwheels.

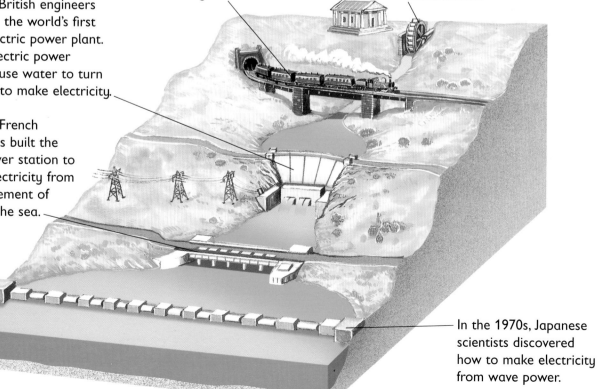

In the 1970s, Japanese scientists discovered how to make electricity from wave power.

Try This! Make a Waterwheel

You will need:
a cork
a plastic bottle
a pair of scissors
a plastic flowerpot
2 small, thin knitting needles
a jug and some water

You will need to ask an adult to help you with this activity.

ASK
AN
ADULT

1 Cut six rectangles, all the same size, from the plastic bottle. The rectangles should be the same length as the cork.

2 Now cut six slits in the cork. Slide the plastic rectangles into each one to make the blades.

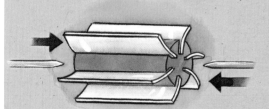

3 Push a knitting needle into the middle of each end of the cork.

4 Cut two slots, opposite each other, into the plastic flower pot. Place the needles in the slots to balance the cork and blades over the center of the flowerpot.

5 Place the flowerpot in a plastic container (to catch the water). Now pour your jug of water slowly over the blades and watch them turn.

As water is poured on the blades, it turns the wheel.

Try pouring the water from different heights. Do the blades turn at different speeds if the water is poured from different heights?

YOU CAN TRY THIS!

Read all about it!

NARRAGANSETT TIMES

Dateline Summer 1859

Pleasure Trip Nightmare!

Teenager Ida Zoraidia Lewis (17) is today being called a heroine throughout the USA. Yesterday she rescued four boys from the rough waters of Narragansett Bay, Massachusetts. A pleasure trip turned to nightmare when their sailboat capsized.

By our East Coast Reporter

Hearing cries for help, Ida launched her own row boat. She reached the panic-stricken boys within minutes and pulled them to safety. In spite of her small frame, Ida is as strong as many men and perhaps braver than most!

panic-stricken boys pulled to safety

Ida is no stranger to the wild winds and waves of Narragansett Bay. Twice a day, in all weathers, she rows the 300 yards across the bay to ferry her two young brothers and her sister to school.

Young Ida Lewis is a heroine in other ways. For the past two years, ever since her father fell ill, she has done his job as lighthouse-keeper. Daily, she climbs the hundreds of steps to the top of the lighthouse tower to clean and fill the huge oil lantern that sends lifesaving warning signals to sailors out at sea. She cares for both her invalid parents, and her brothers and sister, too. More than enough for one young girl, you might think. But Ida's energy seems boundless.

lifesaving warning signals to sailors out at sea

Ida's next challenge is to become the first official woman lighthouse keeper in the whole world!

▲ Try writing your own newspaper article about a dramatic rescue at sea.

During her life, Ida Lewis saved 18 lives — the last when she was 64 years old. In 1879, she was awarded a Gold Medal for bravery. She was also officially appointed lighthouse keeper, after doing the job unofficially for over 20 years.

Water Travel

Water travel is one of the oldest forms of transport. People have traveled on the sea since about 50,000 B.C. The first boat was probably a floating log powered by people paddling with their hands. Ever since, boats have been developed and improved. They have been powered by paddle, wind, steam, and oil.

YOU CAN TRY THIS!

Floating and Sinking

Boats can be made from heavy materials, such as wood, iron, and steel. They are often loaded with heavy cargoes. So how do they stay afloat? These experiments will help you find out.

Staying Afloat

You will need: a metal bottle top, a large bowl, water

1 *Fill the bowl half full of water.*

2 *Drop the bottle top into the water so it hits the water with its side, not its top or bottom. Write down what you see.*

3 *Now take the bottle top out of the water. Dry the top and lay it gently on the top of the water. What happens?*

Time Line *– from paddle to modern supertanker*

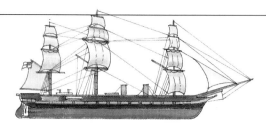

Egyptian ship, 1500 B.C. Chinese junk, 1200   *Mayflower*, 1620   Early steamship, 1860

Why boats float

Objects will only float if they are less dense, or less heavy for their size, than water.

When the bottle top is dropped into the water side-first, it fills with water. This makes it more dense than the water, so the bottle top sinks. When the top is laid carefully onto the water, it fills with air, not water.

Air weighs less than water, so this time the top is light for its size and less dense than the water, so it floats.

Boats are like the empty bottle top. They are made from heavy materials, but they have lots of air inside them. This makes them less dense than water, so they float.

Sinking and rising

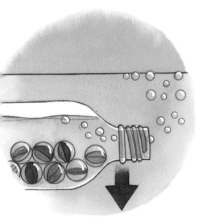

Submarines do not always float on water like other boats. Instead, they sink and travel beneath the surface of the water. Unlike other boats, they can change from being denser than water to being less dense.

You will need: an empty plastic bottle, marbles, plastic tube, water bowl, water

1 *Put the bottle into the water. Put enough marbles into the bottle to make it start to sink.*

2 *As the bottle sinks, more water will flow into it. Air bubbles will come out of the bottle. The air bubbles will rise to the surface as the water replaces the air inside the bottle.*

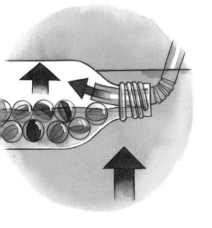

3 *To make the bottle rise to the surface, you will need to fill it up again with air. Push one end of the plastic tube into the bottle and blow. When you have blown enough air into the bottle, it will start to rise to the surface.*

Submarines use air chambers to sink and rise in this way.

Aircraft carrier, 1944, powered by oil

Oil tanker, 1999, powered by oil

Water Sports

There are lots of ways to have fun on or in the water! People of all ages enjoy water sports. Some sports are slow and graceful, others are fast and wild. Do you enjoy swimming? Or perhaps you have been sailing or windsurfing?

Water Sports Records

Fastest speed on water: Kenneth Warby (Australia), 345 mph (555 kph) in 1977.

World's biggest swimming pool: In Casablanca, Morocco, 1,575 ft (480 m) long x 246 ft (75 m) wide.

Fastest swimmer: Tom Jager (USA), 5.370 mph (8.640 kph) in 1990.

First solo round-the-world sailor: Francis Chichester (UK) in 1967.

How many different ways are people enjoying water in this picture?

Did you know...

Most famous romance on water:
In 47 B.C., Queen Cleopatra of Egypt sailed down the **Nile River** in a barge with perfumed sails to meet Roman army commander Mark Antony.

Largest amount of money raised for charity by a sponsored swim:
£122,983.19 ($198,372) in Scotland in 1992. 3,218 swimmers took part.

Walking on water:
In 1987, David Kiner (USA) walked 96 mi (155 km) along the Hudson River with "skijacks" (small water skis) strapped to his feet.

Walking across water:
In 1859, French acrobat Charles Blondin became the first person to walk on a tightrope across Niagara Falls — a distance of about 1,000 ft (305 m).

A lifetime of water sport:
Fritz Lindner (Germany) paddled 64,266 mi (103,423 km) by canoe between 1928 and 1987.

Highest waves ridden by surfers: 50 ft (15.25 m) in Hawaii, in the Pacific Ocean.

Youngest water-sports world-record holder: Gertrude Ederle (USA), aged 12, for freestyle swimming in 1919.

World record high diver: Oliver Favre (Switzerland), 174 ft 36.7 in (53 m 93.4 cm) in 1987.

Water Music, Water Art

◆ *This painting is by the French artist Claude Monet (1840–1926). He captured the shimmering stillness of the water and showed how the water reflects all around.*

Tumbling waterfalls, sparkling fountains, deep, shining pools — water often looks very beautiful. Beautiful water has inspired many poems, pieces of music, and works of art.

You could make a piece of water art of your own. You could show water gushing upward in a fountain, pouring down like a waterfall, or still and shiny, reflecting the sky. If you need inspiration, use the poem on the opposite page to give you some ideas.

Try making a collage and use as many shiny, sparkly materials as you can find to make your picture look like water. Or wet a piece of paper all over and then paint a water scene and see what happens.

Try This! Water Music

You can make musical instruments from glass bottles filled with water.

1 Play your water bottle by blowing across the top of it. You can change its note by changing the water level inside.

2 Play a water orchestra by tapping glass bottles of water with a metal spoon. Adjust the water level inside each bottle to give a different note.

If you know how to play the recorder, try playing this tune. It is by George Frideric Handel (1685-1759), and comes from a collection of pieces known as Handel's *Water Music*.

➥ *Handel wrote this* Water Music *to entertain King George I of England and his guests at a royal boating party in 1740. It was originally played by flutes, trumpets, and drums.*

THE FOUNTAIN

Into the fountain
    Full of the light,
Leaping and flashing
    From morning till night!

Into the moonlight
    Whiter than snow
Waving so flower-like
    When the winds blow!

Into the starlight,
    Rushing in spray,
Happy at midnight,
    Happy by day!

Ever in motion
    Blithesome and cheery,
Still climbing heavenward,
    Never a-weary;

Glad of all weathers
    Still seeming best
Upward or downward
    Motion thy rest;

Full of a nature
    Nothing can tame,
Changed every moment,
    Ever the same;

Ceaseless aspiring
    Ceaseless content,
Darkness or sunshine
    Thy element;

Glorious fountain!
    Let my heart be
Fresh, changeful, constant,
    Upward like thee!

James Russell Lowell

What's More...

More on Floating and Sinking

Look back at pages 22 and 23 to see some experiments on floating and sinking. As the bottle top experiment shows, the air inside the bottle top (and the air in boats) helps it to stay afloat. There is another reason why boats float. The water helps them by pushing upward from underneath.

When boats float in the water, they push some of the water out of the way. This is called displacement. But the water tries to push back again. This is called buoyancy. Displacement and buoyancy are always equal. Together, they keep boats floating in the water.

Did you know...

Buoyancy and displacement were discovered over 2,000 years ago by an ancient Greek scientist named Archimedes. He noticed how the water level rose when he got into his bath, and how it fell when he got out again. He was so excited by his discovery that he leapt out of his bath and rushed out of the house to tell his fellow scientists all about it!

Try This! Nor Any Drop To Drink!

Water, water everywhere,
And all the boards did shrink.
Water, water everywhere
Nor any drop to drink!

This verse is from a poem called "The Ancient Mariner." It was written by Samuel Taylor Coleridge, who lived about 200 years ago. It tells the story of a mariner (sailor) who was shipwrecked in the middle of the sea.

He was surrounded by salty sea water, but had no fresh water to drink. Can you imagine how you would feel if you were surrounded by water but you were unable to drink it?

Write a poem to express your imaginary feelings. You might like to start with the words "Water, water everywhere...," or you could use all your own words.

"Breathing" in Water

Substances such as sugar are not the only things that dissolve in water (*see page 8*). Oxygen, the gas we breathe in, also dissolves in water.

This is important for some water creatures. Many types of fish breathe the oxygen in the water. Mammals, such as whales (*see pages 14–15*) and dolphins, have to come to the surface of the water and breathe the oxygen from the air, like we do.

40 percent of fish live in fresh water; 60 percent live in the sea.

➤ *A blue whale and its young.*

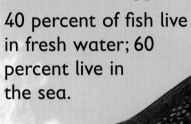

More Water Sports Records

Oldest surviving boat:
A canoe made around 6315 B.C., in the Netherlands.

Longest yacht race:
Vendée Globe Challenge, around the world (22,500 miles or 36,209 kilometers). Fastest time = 109 days in 1955.

First swimmer to cross the Atlantic Ocean:
Benoit Leconte (French) in 1998.

Greatest number of Olympic medals for water sports:
Mark Spitz (USA), 9 gold, one silver, and one bronze for swimming, between 1968 and 1972.

Number Work

Using the information here and on pages 24-25, try to work out the following math puzzles.

✪ How much faster is the world's fastest boat than the world's fastest swimmer?

✪ Assuming that yachts in the Vendée Round-the-World Challenge sail at the same speed all the time, how far do they travel each day?

✪ How old is the world's oldest boat?

✪ How long ago was the first around-the-world voyage?

Glossary

broadscale flood: A flood caused by rain falling for a long time over a wide area.

cartilage: Rubbery tissue found at the end of bones in humans and other animals. It forms the whole skeleton of some sea creatures, such as sharks.

clam: A sea creature, found buried in sand, that lives inside a two-part shell. It has a single foot, which helps it move, and a breathing tube, which helps it survive under the sand. Most clams are small, but a few can grow to about 20 ft (15 m) long. Some are edible.

cockle: A small sea creature, found in shallow water, that lives inside a two-part shell. There are over 250 different varieties; some are edible.

condensation: Water droplets that have condensed (turned to a liquid).

condense: To turn from water vapor into liquid water. This usually happens when water vapor cools.

dense: Heavy for its size.

disinfectants: Chemicals that are used to kill germs.

dissolve: When a solid or a gas mixes together with a liquid. Often, it seems to disappear. The resulting mixture is called a solution.

drought: Period of time when less rain falls than usual, and there is a shortage of water.

flash flood: A flood caused by a sudden heavy downpour of rain.

generator: A machine used to turn the energy contained in oil, coal, wind, or waves into electric power.

hydroelectric power: Electricity made from waterpower.

hydrosphere: All the water on or near the earth's surface.

mammal: A group of animals that feed their young with milk from their own bodies.

Number work answers

page 14: Highest and lowest creatures live 9 mi (15 km) apart; a swordfish travels 58.5 mph (94.2 kph) faster than a blenny; you get 67 pygmy gobly; a blue whale weighs 0.25 tons per foot/meter

page 29: The boat is 339.50 mph (546.36 kph) faster; the yachts travel at 137 mi (220.6 km) a day; the boat is 8,314 years old; the voyage was 32 years ago.

30

Glossary

ocean current: A stream of water that flows within an ocean. Movement between ocean currents and the atmosphere (air around us) can affect the world's weather.

plankton: Very tiny plants and animals that float in seawater.

reservoir: A large tank, pool or lake used to store water.

saliva: Liquid produced by special glands in people's mouths. It helps digest food.

sea anemone: Jelly-like sea creature that lives on rocks and in rock pools. It uses tentacles to catch plankton and other food. The largest sea anemone can be about 3 ft (1 m) wide.

steam: Clouds of water vapor.

tentacles: Finger-like parts of several different sea creatures, including octopuses and sea anemones.

turbine: A machine, usually powered by steam, that produces electricity.

ultraviolet light: Rays of light coming from the sun that cannot be seen by human eyes (though they are visible to some insects). Ultraviolet rays can cause serious sunburn. They can be used to kill dangerous germs.

water cycle: The continuous movement of water from seas and oceans into the earth's atmosphere and back down again to the ground as rain, hail, or snow.

water-treatment plant: A factory where water is cleaned and made safe to drink.

water vapor: Water that has turned into a vapor (gas) by heating. Water vapor is made up of tiny water droplets floating in the air. Water turns from a liquid to a gas when it is heated.

Index